MURPHY'S COMPUTER LAW

D5

Murphy's Computer Law

or

if anything can go wrong it will,
and nothing will go wrong like a computer

JOACHIM GRAF

translated from the German by
Rosemary Dear

with illustrations by
Rolf Boyke

SOUVENIR PRESS

English language edition first published 1994 by
Souvenir Press Ltd, 43 Great Russell Street,
London WC1B 3PA
and simultaneously in Canada

ISBN 0 285 63228 0

Photoset by Rowland Phototypesetting Ltd,
Bury St Edmunds, Suffolk

Printed in Great Britain by
The Guernsey Press Co. Ltd, Guernsey, Channel
Islands

CONTENTS

Acknowledgement

I am particularly indebted to the German and international computer industry. Without them this book would never have been written.

Disclaimer

Any resemblance in this book to living people, existing firms, current products, available brands or actual sales strategies is not intentional, but unavoidable.

Dedication

To my wife Gerti, as well as Sven, Lars and Manuel for their daily suggestions for the chapter 'People', and my partner Daniel Treplin for the chapter 'Computer freaks'.

Preface

Perhaps no field of research has contributed more to the understanding of our modern industrial and communications society than Murphy's Law. Anyone who has realised that anything that can go wrong will go wrong will have acquired a deeper understanding of the world, of life and of everything else.

The practical applications of Murphy's Law extend from 'A' for 'Atomic Industry' ('The more dangerous and absurd a project is, the more passionately will politicians support it') to 'Z' ('When you want to describe something from A to Z you will find no example for either "A" or "Z"'). Murphyological research has produced a wealth of published literature.

For almost every source of day-to-day problems—be it women or the current government—murphyological studies are now available. But for reasons incomprehensible to the author, one area has so far been overlooked: electronic data processing (EDP).

Unlike most things, computers are insidious objects that subject our daily lives to greater and greater heights of Murphy's Law. Every problem-bearing component imaginable has now been incorporated into the computer system: central processing unit, monitor, mass storage, expansion cards, keyboard and other peripherals, all striving for maximum mutual incompatibility. As if this were not enough, the trinity of programmer, program and user also has the guaranteed support of Nature's Law of Entropy, by which Nature constantly aspires to a state of the greatest possible chaos.

The present volume is an attempt to fill this gap in murphyological research.

The author has put to good use his years spent working with computer systems as a user, programmer and journalist specialising in EDP— always as a loser.

Should the reader discover a technical error or a spelling mistake in the book, this too is the work of Murphy's Law. Because:

1 the author has done his best to avoid these errors, and
2 this book has been produced by a computer with a word processing program and corrected by an automatic spell check program.

A BASIC MURPHYOLOGICAL PRINCIPLES

Murphy's Law is a precise and logical development of the general Law of Entropy, by which all particles in the universe try to arrange themselves in the greatest disorder possible. The acknowledgement that these particles go out of their way to trip you up at least once is expressed in

Murphy's Law

If anything can go wrong, it will.

With the invention of computers mankind tried for the first time to endow inanimate matter with a certain intelligence. A fatal decision: so far computers have been neither intelligent nor creative. However, they have already got treachery, subterfuge and cunning down to a fine art. So we can expand Murphy's Law with the

First digital deduction

Computers obey Murphy's Law like nothing else.

But since the modern computer is now more than just a piece of equipment that can perform many tasks simultaneously, this implies the

Second digital deduction

Everything goes wrong at least once.

With the invention of check totals, correction and back-up programs as well as error-tolerant systems, mankind—now downgraded to the status of a mere object—has, in astonishment at the versatility of electronic data processing, been forced to develop the

Third digital deduction

Things go wrong even when absolutely nothing can go wrong.

If we analyse the wealth of experience of users, programmers, developers and other poor devils we can now apply Murphy's Law and its digital deductions to everyday electronic life:

First electronic application of Murphy's Law

With computers, anything can be done and anything is possible—except when you want it.

Second electronic application of Murphy's Law

In the world of EDP, problems never end, they just overlap.

Third electronic application of Murphy's Law

Computer problems wait patiently for the most inconvenient moment, then strike without mercy.

Daniel's query about the third electronic application
Can a problem 'strike'?

The author's answer to Daniel's query
You just watch 'em!

Fourth electronic application of Murphy's Law

When it comes to computers there are no certainties—not least because there are no certainties.

Fifth electronic application of Murphy's Law

1 You can never extricate yourself from a big problem by creating a small one.
2 At best the smaller problem amalgamates with the bigger one for moral support.

Sixth electronic application of Murphy's Law

Nobody can ever imagine just how many problems lurk inside a computer.

Bernard's lamentation
But you can be sure that each one will give you a headache.

Bernard's conclusions
1 Really big problems behave like TV directors: they put on as many repeats as possible.
2 There is no such thing as a cheap problem.
3 If you do have a cheap problem, then you have underestimated its real extent.

Since computers and electronic data processing probably originally had something to do with mathematics, this general introduction to computer-murphyology would not be complete without the mathematical basis of Murphy's Law. The reader should take into account that mathematics, binary logic and human logic on the one hand and EDP equipment on the other have absolutely nothing in common. Unless, of course, you try to prove the following:

Mathematical basis for Murphy's Law

The exact mathematical formula for Murphy's Law in the sphere of EDP is expressed as: $1+1=2$, where '$=$' is a symbol with the meaning 'rarely, if ever'.

Deviation theorem

The difference between digital logic and Murphy's Law is that in digital logic you must work from the premise that everything always goes wrong in the same way.

Binary translation of the deviation theorem
If 0 is particularly big, then it is almost as big as a small 1.

B WINNERS

Wherever a computer and a human being get together there will be a winner and a loser. Which is the winner and which the loser is a foregone conclusion: no matter what happens, the human being is always the loser. In computing as in life it always comes down to the

General law of the loser

It doesn't matter which side you are on—that side will lose.
If you change sides, the flow of battle will also swing the other way.

The general law of the loser, as it applies to, and defines, EDP, results in the

Digital rule of four

1 If you are a user, then the computer, the hardware manufacturer and the programmer will win.
2 If you are a hardware manufacturer, then the computer, the user and the programmer will win.
3 If you are a programmer, then the computer, the hardware manufacturer and the user will win.

Definition of owners of 'home' and 'semi-professional' computers:
A male being who doesn't mind sacrificing endless hours on an activity which is of no practical use, thereby losing his grip on reality so that he no longer has time for his surroundings, his fellow men, his friends or his family.

Conclusions consistent with the digital rule of four
1   There can be no human winners.
2   The computer always wins.

Expanded conclusion from the digital rule of four
Should the computer lose, then the software or the peripherals will win, or at least the electric socket.

On the basis of these deductions we shall deal in the following chapters with the winners in the general battle of life: computer hardware and software.

Every computer owner knows that it is not just the injustices of technology that lie in wait for him. If he is unlucky enough to share his home or office with people as well as a computer, he faces further dangers from 'friends', neighbours, colleagues and relatives. In short: the combination of malicious technology and computer amateurs causes even more havoc.

In chapter 4, however, the general law of the loser will be extended to non-computer owners: there the author is interested in analysing the laws which—according to normal people—result from bumping into a computer freak.

1.0 Hardware

Hardware is the successful attempt to foresee errors in software, to make the most of existing errors and to accumulate and manufacture them with ever greater speed.

Hardware consists of the computer, the keyboard, the printer and the disk capacity, as well as all the other cunning devices etched on silicon.

From the user's point of view, the role of hardware is to produce perfectly, and with the greatest possible speed, the greatest possible number of uncorrectable faults in the shortest possible time, corresponding to the given commands.

For programmers and manufacturers, however, the role of hardware is to produce perfectly and with the greatest possible speed, the greatest possible number of uncorrectable faults in the shortest possible time, corresponding to the given commands.

Double law of complex hardware

1 Complex systems have a tendency to produce complex faults.
2 On the other hand, simple systems have a tendency to produce complex faults.

First expansion
New systems produce new faults.

Second expansion
New systems repeat their new faults.

Third expansion
Old systems produce both new and old faults.

Conclusions

1 Complex systems have a tendency to obstruct their own function.
2 Computers only function so that they can produce faults.
3 Systems have a tendency to grow and therefore get above themselves.

The department-specific deduction

If you want a permanent excuse in your department for your own faults, then you must equip yourself with a computer (see also APPENDIX F: THE BEST EXCUSES.

First contrast between digital and analog logic

People who work with computers do not behave as the computer demands they should.

Second contrast between digital and analog logic

People will behave sensibly when, and only

when, all other possibilities have been exhausted.

Third contrast between digital and analog logic

Foolproof systems are only used by fools.

Contrast between digital and digital logic

Computers which work with other computers do not behave as the other computers demand they should.

The assembly axiom

Everything that is put together falls apart sooner or later.

Aggravations
1 Everything falls apart sooner . . .
2 . . . and always at the most inconvenient moment.
3 All inanimate objects go out of their way to get in the way.

General laws of repair

1 If you can find the part that is faulty then you can't find the tool to remove it.
2 If you do manage to remove it, then the computer retailer has to send it back to the manufacturer.
3 If the retailer does have a replacement in stock, it will not be needed.
4 The cost of repairs can be determined by mul-

tiplying the estimate for the cost of repairs and the price of a new piece of equipment by two and taking the higher of the two values.

5   A spare part supplied by a retailer is not compatible with your computer.

6   Likewise a repaired part is no longer compatible once it has been put back.

7   If a hard disk has to be repaired you will never see the data stored on it again.

Exception to the seventh law of repair
All you will be able to restore on the hard disk is the list of file names so that you can see what has been lost.

The manufacturer's timing dilemma
('EISA-Syndrome')

1   If you promote a product too early, then everyone will have forgotten about it by the time it finally appears.

2   If you promote it too late, then the competition will produce a similar one more quickly.

3   It is always too early or too late.

Consequences (also known as 'Jack's disaster')

1   New products will be promoted earlier and earlier, at least six months before the completion of the first prototypes.

2   Products will always appear after the advertised launch date, at the earliest six months after the advertising campaign.

3   As soon as a piece of equipment is actually

24

1 Taking a piece of equipment apart is simple.
2 Putting it back together again so that it still works is impossible.

available it becomes obsolete.

4 The actual launch of a product on the market always comes after the competition has started advertising the next generation.

Logical consequence
At all times manufacturers as a whole will continue to advertise existing models to save themselves development and production costs.

Frank's law of options

1 If a manufacturer says that his equipment has this or that option, it means he has deliberately left out an important master disk which must be purchased separately.
2 Expanding it will cost more than the original equipment.
3 The expanded equipment will work, but not for you.
4 If you ever want to sell your computer system you will not be able to get rid of the expanded equipment.

Jim's DIY observations

1 To take a piece of electronic equipment apart is simple.
2 To put it back together again so that it still works is impossible.
3 Kicking it only works for other people.

1.1 Computers

The power of a computer is measured by its intelligence and also by the number of inbuilt errors, the speed with which it can produce the greatest possible number of catastrophes and its response time—that is, the time it takes to recover from your input.

Over the years the computer industry has succeeded in expanding the power and error susceptibility of its systems so that an ever-increasing number of support engineers, repair businesses, installation specialists and trouble-shooting experts can earn a crust. In comparison with this growing market is the ever-decreasing number of firms which are still able to remain in the black without a computer. Not to mention the ever-decreasing number of firms which are still able to remain in the black in spite of their computer.

As we have discovered, Murphy's Law—that anything that can go wrong will go wrong—is demonstrated at its best by the computer. Since the Law is valid both for the computer system and for the 'computers/rest of the world' relationship, there is a good chance that before long there will only be computer manufacturers and computer repair firms left in business, until they too file for bankruptcy on the grounds of obligatory computer errors and a single company remains consisting of nothing but computer errors.

The law of the final price

It is irrelevant how expensive you estimate a computer system to be. In the end it will always be more expensive than expected.

Platt's calculation of the law of the final price
(also known as 'common expansion fever')

$$C > (Y* (1000 + A/15)) + (1.5* B) + A/20$$

where C is the overall cost for Y years, if the user has an annual net income A and imagines that his system will cost B pounds.

Example of Platt's calculation of the law of the final price
An MS-DOS computer, which the salesman says will cost £800, will cost a user with an annual net income of £14,400, including a year's software, training, computer manuals and magazines as well as essential expansion, a total of at least £3,280:

$$(1* (1360)) + (1200) + 720$$

The miracle of size

Every computer is too small.

More specifically
1 If it has a big enough hard disk the main memory will be too small.
2 If it has a big enough main memory the hard disk will be too small.

The MS-DOS expansion of the miracle of size

If the hard disk and main memory are big enough, then it needs an operating system which
a) does not support one or both
b) needs a storage allocation which the available user program does not understand.

The physical expansion of the miracle of size

1 In either case your computer will have one slot too few.
2 You will not discover this until you have bought a new expansion card.

The BIOS observation

1 BIOS is never more than 99 per cent compatible.
2 That last one per cent is the program you use most, which crashes with the loss of data.

The polystyrene prediction

a) The simpler the instructions (e.g. 'pull here'), the harder it is to get all the separate parts out of the packaging.
b) The most important part is always the one thrown away with the packaging.
c) You will not get all the individual parts back in the box when it is packed up to be put away.
d) Once you have taken the computer out of its packaging you will not get it back in.

The quantitative relationship of the polystyrene prediction

The more packing material used

a) the more parts can be damaged whilst unpacking,

b) the more parts cannot be found.

Norman Mailer's observation

Computers are the most intelligent idiots there are.

The 13 laws of components

1 An expensive chip, protected by a fast-working fuse, will protect the fuse by blowing first.

2 Components function until, and only until, they have passed the delivery inspection.

3 You will have removed all 16 support screws from the computer casing before you find out that you have removed the wrong cover.

4 After a cover has been secured with 16 screws you will find that you have forgotten to connect a lead.

5 Once the computer is working again you will find some parts left over on the work bench.

6 Tolerances will accumulate in one direction just to cause the greatest possible difficulty during installation.

7 The slots or chip sockets into which you want to plug or install something are practically inaccessible.

8 For all complicated assembly jobs you need three hands.

It always takes twice as long as
planned to complete a program.

9 For all simple assembly jobs you need four hands.

10 Holes drilled in the casing are one tenth of a millimetre too small.

11 Holes of the right diameter are drilled in the wrong place.

12 Nuts never fit on spare screws.

13 The only available slot is too short to install an expansion card.

The plain truth about batteries

The power-pack of a laptop runs out one minute before you are next due to save.

Relationship between battery and work
The more unstored text you have, the faster the laptop power-pack runs down.

The axiom of private use

The computer which functions perfectly by day will crash at night if you go back to the office to use it for your own private business.

Expansion
But the host will still note down your actions and your boss, contrary to all expectations, will find time to read those protocols.

The law of after-sales service

Computers which have broken down will work while the service engineer is present.

Jorrock's law of servicing
1 If it would be cheaper to buy a new computer, the firm will insist on repairing it.
2 If it would be more convenient to repair the old system, the firm will insist on the newest model.

Segrave's double law of compatibility
1 All PCs are compatible. It's just that some are more compatible than others.
2 Yours is always just that vital bit less compatible.

The law of improvement
1 A computer model is described as 'enhanced', 'advanced' or 'extended' if the manufacturer manages to put right some of the errors which made the preceding version useless.
2 This model will not appear on the market until you have bought the preceding version.
3 Every manufacturer will have included in his improved model enough errors to make at least one more 'improved' version necessary.

1.2 Input Equipment

The computer industry uses keyboard, mouse, trackball and digitiser rather than 'user interface'. Which means basically, if you apply Murphy's Computer Law, that it would be a mistake for the user to think that he can work reasonably with any of this equipment.

Whilst a keyboard means that you can select incomprehensible commands from confused menus with illogical cursor movements that would have been better done by a mouse, the mouse, trackball and digitalising board are used to select incomprehensible commands from confused menus with illogical mouse, trackball and digital pen movements that would have been better done by a keyboard, thereby separating subject and object by such a long and complicated sentence structure that it will make the editor, reader and word-processing program dizzy.

Which is why the forward-thinking computer user is waiting for the first speech-operated input equipment. Only then will it be possible to attain the highest level of misunderstanding between computer and user.

The fundamental keyboard observation

1 Your keyboard always has one less key than your favourite program needs.
2 Your keyboard always has one key too many, which can and will go wrong.

The basic mouse observation on compatibility

If you buy a mouse-system compatible with a three-key mouse, you will never find a single program that uses these three keys. As soon as you change to a Microsoft-compatible two-key mouse you will have to work mainly with a program which needs the third key.

The basic digitiser observation

It doesn't matter how long you have had your digitiser: the surface on the most important functions is so scratched that you regularly get them mixed up.

The basic barcode pen observation

With your barcode pen you will be able to read in everything that is unimportant and error-free— from the label on your jacket to the price of cornflakes. But it will be totally defeated by the barcodes which your program prints out, and will make the greatest number of errors possible.

The trackball/mouse distinction

1   You always have so much space on your desk for a mouse that you go to the trouble of buying a trackball.
2   You never have enough space on your desk for your mouse.

The mouse drive axiom

The mouse drive fails on the only program for which you needed to buy a mouse.

The sausage finger phenomenon

If you hit two keys at the same time the character you don't want will appear on the monitor.

The AT/XT relationship

If you have a keyboard which can operate in two modes it will always be set to the wrong one.

Law of the bouncing escape key (also known as the 'XT-AT-MF2 divergence' or the ' "SHIFT" / "<" and <ESC> bafflement')

If you work with two computers the layout of the keyboards will be totally different.

Law of pull-down menus

1 You always click on one option too far.
2 If there are two wrong options to choose from, the mouse will click on the one which causes the most problems and which will take the most time to return to the original menu.

Greg's lamentation
The key you use most is always the one which packs up—always the E or the space-bar, but never the Pause or the F12 key.

The return supplement to Greg's lamentation
If the return key doesn't work, it is the one on the alphanumeric keyboard, never the one on the numeric keyboard.

Exception
When you are working mainly with the mouse and only need the keyboard to type in long columns of figures, it's the other way round.

The interface phenomenon

The mouse always gets stuck in the interface that is not controlled by the mouse drive.

The law of the 'exit'-'no' double strike

Should you accidentally hit the combination of keys that ends your program you will also hit the key which gives a negative answer to 'Do you wish to save the changes?'

1.3 Printers

A printer consists of a print head which is always jamming, a sheetfeed which is too small, a cable that doesn't fit, a worn-out ribbon or an empty ink cartridge and electronics that are not understood by the computer—and that's just when you switch it on.

In addition to this the printer is the computer's last chance to produce errors. This gives rise to the fulfilment of Murphy's Law in

The last resort of the print-out

1   If everything else has worked the printer will break down.

2 If the printer does not break down then the print-out will be wrong.
3 If the print-out is correct you will not be able to decipher it.
4 If everything goes right, no one will be interested in your print-out anyway.

There are two kinds of printer which will be dealt with simultaneously in this chapter: the dot matrix which covers paper in unreadable hieroglyphs with nerve-racking noise, and the laser printer which does it with nerve-racking speed.

Arnold's printer principle

A print-out is never perfect.

The manuscript proof of Arnold's printer principle
You won't discover the errors in a print-out until you read the copy. By then the print-out will already be in the post.

The graphics proof of Arnold's printer principle
1 The print-out never fits on one page.
2 If it does, then the paper has slipped so that the print-out goes over the perforations.

The mathematical printer-paper proof
For any printed text of length n sides, the amount of paper you have left is n-1 sheets.

The no rhyme or reason syndrome (also known as the 'common label trick')

A printer will print labels without difficulty as long as you are watching it. The moment you leave the room the labels will jam in the paper feed.

The three resolution propositions

1 'High resolution' means a circle on the screen looks like Stonehenge from the air—only smudged.
2 'Medium resolution' means a circle on the screen looks like Stonehenge from the air—only blurred.
3 'Low resolution' means a circle on the screen looks like Stonehenge from the air—only messier.

The Epson law of printer performance

1 'Near letter quality' means that the printer has reproduced something on the paper which is very similar to letters of the alphabet.
2 'Letter quality' is the typeface which is only recognisable as coming from a dot matrix printer if you look carefully.
3 'Draft' is the term for an operating mode which
—leaves the paper unmarked if the ribbon is of poor quality, and
—prints something three millimetres high in

light-grey lines if the ribbon is new.
Naturally, both are produced with the greatest possible speed.

Patricia's printer drive analysis

An application program comes with all sorts of diskettes on which there are all sorts of printer drives.

The following statements can be derived from this:
1 Your printer is not compatible with these drives.
2 If any of these drives is compatible with your printer it won't work.
3 If it is available and working, then it isn't compatible with the interface.
4 If it is available, not faulty and is compatible with the interface, then it only uses Ancient Greek characters and prints them in Tibetan triangular format from bottom left to top right.

The general postscript thesis (also known as the 'DDL-directive' or the 'PCL-instruction')

1 The typeface you want is missing.
2 If the typeface is available then the type style you want is missing.
3 If both are available the printer will print it in the wrong size in the wrong place.
4 In all other cases it will display an error message and stop printing.

The specific postscript thesis (also known as the 'thesis of the lowest common multiple')

1 The printer and program will define the post-script standard quite differently.
2 The only font they will both understand is Courier 10 point.

Exception to the specific postscript thesis
Clause 2 is only valid when you don't need this font. If you want to use Courier 10 point the printer and program will unite to convert all ASCII characters to the 'Symbol' font.

Brian's WYSIWYG definition

The French version of WYSIWYG is *Honi soit qui mal y pense* or HSQMYP.

Brian's revised WYSIWYG definition
The English version of WYSIWYG is 'What you see is what you might get'.

The WYSIWYG complication
As soon as you think you are getting near the end of your work, the English version of WYSIWYG becomes 'What you see is what you never get' or WYSIWYNG.

Charles's basic rule

A printer will never be so short of data that it can't mess up at least one sheet of paper with gobbledegook.

Charles's expanded rule

It doesn't matter how much gobbledegook a printer prints—it will always print out at least one extra line.

Charles's sheet feed observation

1 No tractor feed can be expected to draw in sheets one at a time, no single-sheet feed can be expected to draw in continuous paper.

2 In addition to this a tractor feed exists solely to draw in continuous paper crookedly.

3 A single-sheet feed, on the other hand, exists solely to draw in single sheets of paper crookedly.

Murphy's contradiction of Charles's sheet feed observation

The printer takes in the paper cleanly and exactly at the very moment it isn't required.

Rule of the graphics-producing printer

A square which looks like this on the screen:

will look like this when printed by a printer that cannot handle graphics:

```
ZDDD?
3 3
@DDDY
```

whilst a printer that can handle graphics will
print it like this:

The ASCII/Centronics principle of printer standards

The only thing that is standardised between the
various printers is the mains cable.

Corollary for the Anglo/American special case
Of course this standard is not valid for British
plugs and American current.

1.4 Mass Storage

Mass storage malfunctions via disk, tape, hard
disk or Winchester drives just as it is saving
important data.

The difference between the various drives lies
in the access time, which the computer world
defines as the time a drive takes to
a) fail to find the file it is looking for, and
b) break up all the other important files whilst
   searching, so thoroughly that it is easier to
   type these files in again than to repair them.

In a Winchester drive (equipment that exists to shoot files to pieces) intelligence, malice and insidiousness are interrupted by what is called a hard disk control. Amongst other things this ensures that important files, as a matter of principle, are ruined five minutes before the daily back-up and that unimportant files (for example, the README files of programs erased long ago) remain unharmed.

Tape and disk controls fulfil their murphyological purpose by guaranteeing that the tapes or disks on which the only current version of the data is stored are broken or unreadable.

The back-up premises

1 Back-up always takes one more disk than you have available.
2 A back-up program will fail just when you need it.

First deduction
By crashing with the destroyed version of a file the back-up program will overwrite the only secure copy you have left.

Second deduction
When you want to use the back-up you will discover that the only version of RESTORE was on the disk before you formatted it, and nowhere else.

The disk rule

If a disk jams in the drive you will have to use force to get it out. If this damages the drive it would have had to be renewed anyway.

The reading error dogma

A reading error only appears in a file that you really need and which you have no copy of.

The law of file secrecy

When information is confidential the file remains on the disk by mistake. The appropriate security code will have been forgotten.

Expansion of the law of file secrecy
You will accidentally find and read files that have been hidden from you.

Seagate's formatting axiom

You will always format a disk which is already in the drive with the wrong recording density.

To be more precise
1 You will format an HD disk with 360K.
2 You will format a DD disk with 1.2 mega-bytes.

Conclusion
You won't notice that you have formatted a 360K disk with 1.2 megabytes until you have saved

the only version of a vital file onto it and have therefore lost all the data.

Godfrey's first observation of ubiquitous uncertainty

It's only when you have answered Y to the program's question 'Are you sure—Y/N?' (for example, when formatting) that you realise that you aren't sure at all.

Godfrey's aggravated observation of ubiquitous uncertainty

When you check the disk afterwards you realise that you have just erased your most important file.

Basic rule of the inescapability of sticky liquid

(also known as the 'coke and sweet coffee dogma')

You will only knock over a cup or a glass on your desk when there is still something in it.

Conclusions

1   The liquid will, with unerring precision, make straight for the most important disk on your desk.
2   On its way there it will have to cross the one print-out and draft for which no copy or file exists.
3   The stains will make the most important parts of these documents illegible for ever.
4   Having run onto the destination disk the

46

liquid will flow into the write-read opening.

5 If there are several disks to choose from, the liquid will go for the one which has most files on it and whose contents are irreplaceable.

6 The disk can never be read again afterwards.

7 Even if certain files on the disk can still be read they are unimportant (for example, last week's shopping list).

8 A restoration program will make all sectors of the disk readable again. Except the vital ones.

The CHKDSK principle (or the 'dogma of the futility of human aspirations')

a) When you do a CHKDSK on your hard disk the program won't find a single incoherent block.

b) If you do without it there will be thousands.

The 'Speed Disk' expansion of the CHKDSK principle (known as 'Norton's dilemma')
You will first notice the incoherent blocks when you use Speed Disk or another tool which cannot remove these blocks but grabs the opportunity to ruin your disk.

The 3.5 inch rubbish axiom

The little plastic bags in which 3.5 inch disks are packed can only be used to make the rubbish heap bigger.

The disk box laws

1 It is easier to put a disk into a box than to get it out again.
2 The plastic dividers in the disk box are there to hide the disk you want.
3 Alternatively they tip forward the disks you want.
4 A disk is never where you think it is.
5 You will never need the key. Except when you inadvertently lock the box.
6 Disk boxes cannot be stacked.
7 Perversely, they can so long as you don't touch them. Then they will fall over and spill their contents onto the floor.

A word about the healthy effect of disk boxes
If you lock a disk box to move it, the lock will fly open and all the disks will fall out and scatter as far away as possible from each other around the room.

The writing protection labels aphorisms

1 Writing protection labels don't stick properly.
2 Writing protection labels migrate to the most inaccessible places in the disk drive.
3 Writing protection labels don't come off again.
4 Writing protection labels go missing when you inadvertently format an important disk or you have caught a virus.
5 Writing protection labels stick to data disks

when you want to save and the application program cannot forestall these errors.

Expansion of the fifth writing protection labels aphorism
In this case the program will crash and lose the data.

Matthew's Amiga axiom

1 It doesn't matter which disk is in the drive—it is never the system disk.
2 There is only a system disk in the drive when there is already a newer version of the operating system on your booted up hard disk.

The de Lisle lamentation

You will search in vain for a disk that is empty.

Murphy's expansion of the de Lisle lamentation
You will also search in vain for a disk that is full.

Eve's conclusion from Murphy's expansion of the de Lisle lamentation
You will search in vain for every disk.

2.0 Software

Software is the successful attempt to make the most of the errors of computer hardware and to add new errors through development.

Software is composed of drive systems such as word processing, data processing, graphics, spreadsheet and telecommunications programs which are nothing more than manifestations of stealthiness worked up into programs.

From the user's point of view the sole task of computer software, apart from filling the manufacturers' coffers, is to break down easily, responsibly and with the most data throughput such that the greatest possible damage will be caused in the shortest possible time.

What this means for software manufacturers is that financial and personal expenditure on program development and marketing is in inverse proportion to the expenditure needed for product support. The only software that needs no product support is therefore that for which too big and too expensive a product support service was set up before its introduction into the market.

From the point of view of the user, however, there is

The cowboy company's question

Product support? What's that?

A question which, incidentally, no one has yet been able to answer.

Principle for understanding the software industry

All major software developments have come about because of serious program errors.

First conclusion from the software principle
Every program has errors.

Second conclusion from the software principle
Every program always has one more error.

Third conclusion from the software principle
The removal of one error always causes at least two more.

Personal deduction from the software principle
When errors show up, go home.

First logical inversion of the argument from the existence of usefulness

The fact that there are so many small, useful programs proves that there are also a lot of big, useless programs.

Second logical inversion of the argument from the existence of usefulness

The fact that there are so many big, useless programs proves that there are still more small, useless programs since there are more small programs than big ones.

Ben's conclusion
The effectiveness of a program is in inverse proportion to its price.

The expert's observation

You can recognise an expert system because, when told that 'a rose smells better than a cabbage', it draws the conclusion that roses will also make better soup.

Henry Massingham's contradiction of the expert's observation
Artificial intelligence is better than natural stupidity.

Refutation by the author's wife of Massingham's contradiction
Any program for which a programmer claims the quality of artificial intelligence has accumulated in its database so much natural stupidity that it can give a wide variety of intelligent-sounding and utterly wrong answers.

Hazel's observations on computer games programs

1 You always get one point less than you need for a new highest score.
2 If you have played a game so long that nobody can beat you, a friend will play the game for the first time and will effortlessly achieve first place on the high score list.
3 If you are the best, nobody will be interested.

Matthew's observations on computer games

1 The computer game that you bought is not worth the money you paid for it.
2 No computer game is as good as the picture on the packaging.
3 In a games magazine a good critic only says that the editor liked a game. Your taste may be different from his.
4 You only realise this after you've bought it.
5 Your greatest rival always has a better game than you.

The multifunctionality hypothesis

The fewer functions a program has the better it will perform.

Conclusions from the multifunctionality hypothesis
1 The more perfectly a program performs the more thoroughly it will break down.
2 Every other program will break down just as thoroughly.

Derivation for integrated packages

1 The more functions that are described on the back of the packaging, the fewer the program will be able to control.
2 When it says on the packaging, 'For all users', it's of no use to anyone.
3 All the functions for which you bought the program package need a special module for which you have to pay extra.

Double law of the success/development relationship

1 The more work put into developing a program, the less people will buy it.
2 The less work put into developing a program, the more people will buy it and find errors in it.

First conclusion from the success/development relationship
The more errors inherent in a program, the worse the product support.

Second conclusion from the success/development relationship
Only the program that nobody needs runs without errors.

General principle of clearing

Whilst clearing superfluous security files attached to programs, one which is still under guarantee will disappear only to be urgently needed ten minutes later.

Expansion
This principle is valid not only for security files but also for all files.

The original program dilemma

When you urgently need a program, it has been borrowed and the borrower cannot be reached by phone.

The pirated copy extension
If the borrower is reachable by phone, then the program was a pirated copy which he has inadvertently erased from your hard disk.

The problems premises

1 When you urgently need the software hotline your telephone is out of order or the number is engaged.
2 When you get the ringing tone it's the weekend so there is nobody there.
3 If you get the ringing tone and it's a weekday then it's a day on which the hotline itself is not working.
4 At any other time the only man who can help you with your query is either ill or on holiday.

General axiom of urgency

All things are worse under pressure.

Mathematical definition of the general axiom of urgency

$$U = (P^T/S)* (C + A + N)$$

As you can see, the urgency U can have any value you like at any time. P is the number of problems, T the reciprocal value of the remaining time and S the skill of the person entrusted with solving software problems (its values are 0 < S < 1). The number of problems P is an unknown for the general value P > 0. If P is known then the value is P = P + 1.

The value of PT/S is multiplied by the sum C + N + A in which C is the number of computers concerned, A is the number of application programs in the firm and N the number of computers linked in a network within a radius of 100 metres of the person who is trying to solve the software problem.

Expansion by the author's wife of the general axiom of urgency
All things are worse without pressure.

The mainframe equation

If two processes run at the same time, the less important one will take computer time from the more important one.

The basic virus observation

Computer viruses mostly affect 'guaranteed not infected' programs and drive-system disks.

The general virus observation

Just when you think you haven't got a computer virus, you get one.

The deadline virus observation

You get a computer virus just when you least need it.

The partnership virus observation

Only other people get viruses that are guaranteed harmless and easily eradicated.

The geographical virus observation

You always get the sort of computer virus
—which the experts say no longer occurs in this country
—for which there is no virus searching program
—which displays a new quality of insidiousness and destructiveness.

The quantified virus observation

You always have one more virus than you think you have.

The qualified virus observation

The virus that attacks your computer only infects the files for which you have no back-up.

The expanded qualified virus observation
When you have back-ups for all your files the virus infects these as well.

The integrated quantified virus observation
The virus has always infected one more work station than you think.

The recursive virus observation

The virus search program you use will recognise and fight only those viruses which you don't have. It will leave the virus that you do have untouched.

Expansions of the recursive virus observation
1 You won't discover this until you have bought the program.
2 You will be the only person whose newly acquired virus search program is infected with a virus.
3 You will not discover this until you have started.

The supplemented recursive virus observation
A virus search program used in your computer will destroy all text and program files during its search and leave only the virus behind.

It makes no difference which side
you're on, that side will lose.

Conclusion from the supplemented recursive virus observation
In the end, all you will have left on your computer will be the virus.

2.1 Word Processing

Word processing programs are a most successful attempt to get £600 out of unsuspecting people, promising to replace typewriters and Tipp-Ex with about 300 easy-to-learn commands and leaving users free, in spite of the programs, to concentrate on what they really want to write.

As well as the real work of writing, the user with a word processing package can do a number of more useful things—first and foremost, learning to use the word processing program itself. If he or she has any time left after that, it can be spent on using the word processing program to take care of any additional work.

For example, the *Working with Text Modules* (a sort of phrase generator for inserting unnecessary passages of text in places where they don't fit), the *Management of Headers and Footers* (automatically inserting them where they annoy the author and cannot be found by the reader) or the *Mail Merge Function* (with which you can automatically insert out-of-date addresses in unnecessary letters so that half the addresses will be printed wrongly. Over 90 per cent will be returned by the post office marked 'unknown'

and the other ten per cent will be thrown away
by the recipients.)

Valerie's crash/memory relationship

A computer only crashes when you haven't
saved the text for a long time.

Absolute laws of word processing (also called
the WordStar axioms)

1 When you want to erase a word the whole
   line will disappear.
2 When you want to erase a line the whole
   paragraph will disappear.
3 When you want to erase a paragraph the
   whole lot will disappear.
4 When you want to erase the lot, nothing will
   happen.

Conclusion from the WordStar axioms
In none of these cases will it be recoverable.

Frank's law of word exchange (also known as
the 'Microsoft law of ANnoyance)

When you use the function 'Find-Exchange'
you will forget to change the letter case, so
that although the word to be found only has
one capital letter the word used in exchange
will always have two. Therefore, 'Anoyance'
will always be changed to 'ANnoyance', never
'Annoyance'.

Michael's insight into the nature of function keys

When you have got used to a program with a particular combination of function keys, a new version of the program will appear in which they have been altered.

The law of the high number (also described as the 'word-WordStar-rivalry law' or the 'five-nil syndrome')

1   When a new version of a word processing program appears on the market it will show the highest version number of all existing programs.
2   Two weeks later all the other versions will carry this version number.

Lisa's observation
These version numbers tell you nothing about the number of improvements over the old versions.

Mark's intensification of Lisa's observation
1   The more expensive the update on the new version, the less need there is for it.
2   The higher the version number, the more memory it uses.
3   The feature you have been waiting for for years will not be included in the new version.

Just when you think you haven't got a computer virus, you get one.

Axiom of the underhanded printer error

You only find the critical error in your text when you have printed it out and erased the file from the disk.

The invariable rules of text formatting in the desktop publishing program

1 When you want to position your text the last line will no longer fit on the page.
2 If you format your text to the next smallest unit the text will be too short.

The click and move DTP laws (also known as the 'yes, only make one plan' dilemma)

a) If you click on a box on a page lay-out to move it, you will move the text surrounding it.
b) If you click on the text to move it you will merely move the box.
c) If you want to move both you will move the SpeedBar.
d) You cannot cancel any of these since the 'Cancel' function will not work.
e) If you can cancel any of these you will move something else and ruin the whole layout.

2.2 File Management

File management programs and data banks are a most successful attempt to get £600 out of unsuspecting people, promising to replace card indexes with about 300 easy-to-learn commands and leaving users free to try to remember why they wanted a file management program in the first place.

File management programs and data banks are, as the names imply, in the first line of management programs with which you can put off doing things. As is usual with bureaucracies, there is no relationship between what goes in (the records), what comes out (the sorted records, lists or whatever) and the time between the two.

Although this is theoretically applicable in a general form to all programs, for file management programs the following is particularly valid:

The law of time relationships

It doesn't matter how the relationships in your database seem or how they change—everything takes longer than your most pessimistic forecast.

Basically, no program produces as many excuses (in programmer-speak, 'error messages') for not calling up stored data as file management programs and data banks do.

The Zorro law

1 It doesn't matter how big a mask you put on, it always has too few fields.
2 But when you have defined enough fields they will be too short.

Andy's observation of thieving file management

When you get annoyed that you can't extend the length of the fields in your file management program, don't panic. Your program will shorten the length of the fields arbitrarily anyway and thus dispose of all superfluous data.

Bob's rule of data base records

a) A file management program only destroys those records which you need urgently.
b) Where no back-up exists, all records will be destroyed.
c) If a back-up exists, the record there will also disappear.

Law of minimising the amount of information

1 When you want to put n records into a data bank the only available file management program can at best deal with n-1 records.
2 However, the program will only tell you this when you have already keyed in n-2 records.

Ashton-Tate's law of time management in data banks

It doesn't matter what your data bank structure is: the data bank program you need will display the worst sort of time management in sort and search mode. For example, if your records are known to be completely unsorted, your program will merely search the sorted records in a reasonable time.

The address axiom

It doesn't matter how many addresses you have stored in your data bank: the one you are looking for is no longer there, but on a scrap of paper.

Tony's expansion of the address axiom

1 You will never find the piece of paper containing the address.
2 The first colleague you ask for the address will sneer at you as he recites it from memory.
3 Seconds later you will find the piece of paper with the address.
4 If, on the other hand, the address is stored in the data bank, it has either changed in the meantime or the telephone number is wrong.

2.3 Graphics Programs

Graphics programs are a most successful attempt to get £600 out of unsuspecting people, promising to replace pencils, rulers and rubbers with about 300 easy-to-learn commands and leaving users free to concentrate on what they originally wanted to draw.

Into this category come useless paint programs for professional work, useless drawing programs for artistic work, as well as useless CAD programs for every clear-thinking person.

Paint programs reproduce colours faithfully on the screen, badly on the colour printer and not at all on the black and white printer. Drawing and CAD programs, on the other hand, reproduce single colour lines correctly on the screen and badly on both the colour and black and white printers. But all three sorts of program will reproduce what was black or white on the screen as black or black on the printer.

The definition of the undo function

1 The 'undo' function only works so long as you don't need it.
2 At best it cancels the last but one action you carried out. In this case the effect of your last action will be preserved.

Laws of the highly imaginative screen adaptor

1 Ellipses will be portrayed and printed out as zigzag-edged eggs.
2 Zigzag-edged eggs will remain zigzag-edged eggs.
3 A line always begins one pixel to the side.
4 Circles are not circles.
5 A 10 point grid with 32 degree gradient will eventually emerge from the printer as a smudged something or other.
6 All other grids will eventually emerge from the printer as a smudged something or other.
7 All patterns will eventually emerge from the printer as a smudged something or other.
8 A smudged something or other of a certain area will eventually emerge from the printer as geometrically exact and immediately

recognisable as computer graphics, but still a useless something or other.

Exceptions
1 If there is a gap of one pixel between two lines, they will overlap.
2 Circles are circles when (and only when) you wanted to draw an ellipse. Then the printer will print them correctly as ellipses.
3 A shading function only produces even and exactly parallel lines.

Digital rule of solitude

Your graphics program is the only one on the market which
—cannot work with pictures read in by your scanner
—doesn't understand your word processing
—is incompatible with your desktop publishing program.

Consequent continuation of the digital rule of solitude
You only notice this when the bill has been paid.

Axiom of complete filling

1 It doesn't matter how you want to fill your grid or pattern: the program will always find a way to turn the entire screen black.
2 This process is irreversible.
3 If you have double- and triple-checked all the

lines and intersections so that a Fill pattern cannot escape from the shape to be filled, then you will click the Fill tool next to it.

Freeman's text theorem

1 Your graphics program only uses a hideous typeface.
2 A PostScript printer drive is only there for decoration.
3 Just because your Paint program uses a PostScript printer drive doesn't mean that it can read EPS files or print fonts without zigzags.

The observation on standards

Every new graphics program passes off its new picture format as standard, but can only read and write this particular one.

Logical expansion of the observation on standards
If you buy a new graphics program it will be able to do everything—except read the old picture format.

The TIF improvement on the observation on standards
If, however, your graphics program can read a current picture format then it can only do so in its uncommon form. If, for example, it can read TIF files then it can only read the uncommon, uncondensed TIF format.

70

The fate of the conversion program

Instead of a graphics conversion program you can also use the 'Erase' command. The result is the same, or at least it comes to the same thing.

2.4 Spreadsheet Programs

Spreadsheet programs are a most successful attempt to get £600 out of unsuspecting people, promising to replace pocket calculators and sound human understanding with about 300 easy-to-learn commands and functions and leaving users free to concentrate on what they originally wanted to calculate.

The basis of every spreadsheet program is known as the worksheet, whose tiny columns and cells the user must fill with far too many numbers converted into formulae after much expenditure of time and effort, only to discover later what he already knew. Usually spreadsheet programs are divided two-dimensionally into columns and cells. More modern versions of this program now control a three-dimensional representation in which formula errors have an even greater chance of concealing themselves until the greatest possible damage has been done.

Sharp's rule

An error in a formula only comes to light when the flawed results are plausible.

Generalised expansion of Sharp's rule

Flawed calculations are only noticed at the last possible moment and cause the greatest possible damage.

General rule for calculations

A spreadsheet program which produces a correct or pleasant result is lying.

The axiom of whole numbers

When you have to calculate using whole numbers the program will only contain a list of rubbish. For example, speed will only be printed out in American nautical miles per 19 days.

The results premise

Just before a spreadsheet can supply vaguely useful results, the program will switch on its random number generator.

The problem of the pound

You can print out monetary values in dollars, DM and Fijian mussels. But never in pounds.

The Tab Paradox

1 You will not be able to download data from your word processing program to your spreadsheet program and vice versa.
2 A memory-resident cut-out program will crash because of the tabs, if nothing else.

The pie chart theorem

1 It doesn't matter what data you have to process, your program will be the only one that can't cope with that kind of graphical representation.
2 If the appropriate kind of representation is available, then you have set out the whole chart wrongly.

Concretisation of the pie chart theorem
You will be able to plot 300 individual numbers only as a bar chart and one chronological progression only as a pie chart.

Peter's law of the impossibility of desktop presentation

Forget everything that the salesman has told you about VDI drives and laser printable overhead transparencies.

Practical grounds for Peter's law
1 Your spreadsheet cannot process the data in such a way that it will be accepted by your business graphics package.
2 Your business graphics package and your output device will never understand each other.
3 There is no drive for your printer with this spreadsheet.
4 An overhead projector is the most expensive way of finding out that there is yet another error in the graphics. Apart from

that it's a way of presenting the control file in ASCII on a transparency instead of the graphics.

5 When everything is working there is no electricity supply in the presentation room.

6 When you make sure beforehand that there is an electricity supply in the presentation room, the event is cancelled or you forget the vital cable.

7 If everything goes like clockwork, then no one will be interested in your presentation.

2.5 Telecommunications

Telecommunications programs are a most successful attempt to get £400 out of unsuspecting people, promising that with about 100 easy-to-learn commands they will, in spite of the Royal Mail and high telephone charges, be able to get something sensible on their monitor that they couldn't get by other quicker and cheaper means.

Generally there are two main arguments given for using a telecommunications program:

—communication with several users in all sorts of countries via a keyboard (called the 'conference' or the 'chat'), as well as

—the retrieval of information from on-line data banks.

The obvious advantage of a chat over a normal

phone call is first of all that it takes longer and costs more (for the essential exchange of information such as 'hiya folks', 'C U 18th' and ':-)' one must generally pay between five and seven different telephone rates). On the other hand, the critical difference between an on-line data bank and a printed information service, although neither of these will give you what you are looking for, is that it costs far more to find this out via a data bank.

Glover's observation

Telecommunication is the most awkward and involved way of telephoning someone.

The basic on-line rule

Before you can save your message someone always trips over the telephone cable.

First derivation of the basic on-line rule
If you are alone, then the on-line time runs out before you can save.

Second derivation of the basic on-line rule
Your on-line time is just long enough for you to write a long text as far as the last but one character.

Axiom of the query in on-line data banks

Forget everything you have ever heard about standardised queries.

Concrete examples of the query axiom

1   The only commands an on-line data bank responds to are those that you can't think of, in spite of racking your brains for hours.
2   Wrong or wrongly keyed-in commands always attract the highest charges.
3   As far as data bank compilers are concerned, help functions are superfluous.
4   The specimen query quoted in the advertising brochure from a data bank compiler is the only one that works.
5   It only works with the search term quoted. If in the example 'SEARCH car AND parliament' is quoted then a search with terms other than 'car' and 'parliament' will only lead to an expensive error message.

Axiom on the information content of on-line data banks

The amount of information I stored in the on-line data bank can be expressed through the following formula:

$$I = A - L$$

in which A is all the information available on a theme, and L the information you are looking for.

Conclusion
You will find everything in an on-line data bank, except what you are looking for.

The conference dilemma

In a chat, the conference is either full, or there's no one there except you.

Password law

The number of forgotten passwords increases exponentially with the number of your mailbox-user call-signs.

Tom's lamentation
1 You will always forget more passwords than you need.
2 The passwords that you can still remember are the ones you changed last week.

Alec's expansion
When you do remember a valid password, it is valid for another system.

The Prestel rule (also known as the BT phenomenon)

The more absurd a system is, the more subsidies it will receive.

Communications principles

1 If you receive a leaflet about a new telephone or data service available in your area, then your local office will not have heard of it when you ask them about it.
2 If they have heard about it, it will be unavailable.

3 Your telephone bill is always double what it was in your worst nightmares.
4 The only low charges will be for services you don't use—for example, sending telegrams to the Fiji Islands or renting meteorological satellites in geostationary orbit.
5 The words 'CAUTION DATA CARRIER' will prompt the Post Office to put the envelope containing your disks under a magnetic reading device.
6 The words 'DO NOT BEND' will prompt the postman to roll up the envelope with your disk in it and wedge it in your letter box.

Law of recursion

Every really important message which is sent via a mailbox network will mistakenly be identified as a recursion and intercepted by an overzealous program routine.

Expanded law of recursion
But if you have, in your state of exhaustion, typed in a meaningless, ridiculous message full of mistakes, it will still be readable in the whole network hours later.

The network axiom

The mailbox will only notice that your netmail account is empty when you have typed in and sent a long message.

The basic rules of broadcasting speed

1 Too high a baud rate leads to)%'"!/−?&y/-.
2 Your terminal program always uses a baud rate which neither your modem, nor the mailbox calling you, can understand.

Roger's definitive classification of mailbox users

On the basis of years of research in the field, mailbox users can be divided into the following—and for a mailbox operator extremely annoying—categories:

1 BLIND:
   READ * NEW

2 ACTIVE:
   SEND: TEST
   :test
   :
   :quit
   :q
   :bye
   :'Z
   :
   :*%#@*$00 ... carrier lost—restart program

3 PASSIVE:
   <personal mode> Command: − ... Time-out stopping.

4 DETERMINED:
   BULLETIN BOARD/Z-NET/AMIGA/BINARY

```
        READ *
        LOGOFF

5   UNDECIDED:
        ?
        ?
        LOGOUT

6   FUSSY:
        CANCEL *
        BULLETIN BOARD +

7   DISBELIEVING:
        READ 124
        READ 124
        READ 124

8   BEGINNER:
        124
        124
        LOGOFF
        GET OUT
        BYE
        LET'S GET OUT OF HERE
        :*%#@*$00  ...  carrier  lost—restart
        program

9   ADVANCED:
        READ/Z-NET

10  SPECIALIST:
        SEND SYSOP :AUTOEXEC

11  CAUTIOUS:
        SEND SYSOP :I may have a question

12  DYNAMIC:
        SEND SYSOP :THIS IS A LOAD OF CRAP
```

13 LONELY:
   TIME
   It is 03:15:37, you have been in this system
   for 12 minutes
   DIALOGUE
   CO
   LOGOFF

14 PATIENT:
   SEARCH * T :WHAT'S NEW

Roger's definitive Sysop classification

On the basis of years of research in the field,
mailbox operators, on the other hand, fall into
one or more of the following 11—and for a mailbox user extremely annoying—categories:

1 Ascetic: 'I don't want another bulletin board.
   I've already got one.'
2 Spendthrift: 'How many megabytes are
   carried daily on this network? Big deal,
   tomorrow I'm getting a 1200 baud modem.'
3 Finicky: 'LED? Great, I'll just set up a bulletin
   board on this theme.'
4 Boy Scout: 'Search system for exchange of
   /Q–NET/IBM/PROGRAM/GENERAL. Off-peak
   rates, please.
5 Repetitive: 'My new release: C-NET—The
   greatest hits of A-NET and B-NET.'
6 Quick and decisive: 'A /Z-NET ON CHRIST-
   MAS EVE? Great, I'll have one!'
7 Sceptic: '/Z-NET/ENVIRONMENT? Nobody
   was interested 20 years ago and I'm not
   interested now.'

8 Fatalistic: 'What do I want a bulletin board
   for? I'm FIDO-Point.'

9 Optimistic: 'Where there's a bulletin board,
   there's a user.'

10 Trailblazing: 'Where there's a user, can a
   bulletin board be far behind?'

11 Laid-back: 'Whatever's there, I'm not
   bothered.'

3.0 People

According to unconfirmed reports there exists, outside the triangle of computer freak-computer-computer freak, another mysterious world full of non-computer freaks.

This world influences a computer system both directly—through electricity supply, disks or other closely related objects—and indirectly, via computer freaks. The influence manifests itself by alternately activating, encouraging, anticipating, arranging, deducing, intensifying, optimising or concentrating computer errors—and continually harassing the computer user.

Mealtimes will faithfully follow Murphy's Basic Rule by interrupting you right in the middle of developing a brilliant algorithm and driving it out of your head forever, and a child bursting into the room (just like some adults) will tread on all the vital disks.

But kindred spirits themselves—namely, other computer users—are just as talented at causing errors, damage and havoc and this is why (at great inconvenience) they are dealt with in this chapter as well.

Law of structural incompatibility of the wife and the hobby of computing

The one time you are working on a long and unsaved source code, a housewife will use the only appliance for miles around which blacks out the whole area.

The baby-on-your-knee axiom

A child who touches the keyboard immediately hits the only combination of keys by which something is erased. If there is more than one possibility, it will pick the most disastrous.

The restricted baby-on-your-knee axiom
If you do manage to stop the child hitting the disastrous combination of keys, then you will probjcbbbbbbbj,zhfh.j .uik goui oliz okizh.o .gjk.gjk.gk.gk.gk.jgkjgkj.gk.jgkjgkj.g.kjgklkgj.k .gjkgj.gk.j.gkjg.jkgjkgjkgjkgjkgkjgkjgjk

The phenomenon of the interested teenager

The only reason why your children are interested in your computer is that they can copy lots of pirated games onto your hard disk while you are not there.

Conclusion from the phenomenon of the interested teenager
This activity will transport the only virus within a 200-mile radius straight into your computer.

The other-system phenomenon

1 The most experienced computer freak in your neighbourhood will have a different computer system.
2 He will point out to you at every available opportunity that your computer is only bought by absolute beginners.
3 Everyone will believe him.

Refinements on the other-system phenomenon
—If you have an Amiga System you will be laughed at because it's a games computer.
—If you have an Atari System you will be laughed at because it's a would-be graphics computer.
—If you have a Commodore 64 System, you will be laughed at because it's a play-school computer.
—If you have a Macintosh System you will be laughed at because it's cheap and cheerful.
—If you have an MS-DOS System you will be laughed at for being behind the times.
—If you have a work station you will be laughed at for having an unsophisticated operating system.
—If you have another system you will be laughed at for being an eccentric.

Allegory of objectivity in computer clubs

It doesn't matter what kind of computer you use: you never have the newest or the best model and you will always be laughed at in your computer club because of it.

Ginny's hypothesis of the theme adoption of computer clubs

1 Every computer club should set itself up as a properly constituted association if it is to work effectively on topics.
2 Why should it work effectively on topics? There are much more important things to do, such as having club elections, committee disputes and discussions on the constitution.

4.0 Computer Freaks

To describe the subject of this chapter—computer freaks—we must first define what they are not. As an outline definition we can therefore use the

Definition of the computer user

A stressed, usually female, being who has to work with useless programs, incomprehensible manuals and incompatible peripherals at a screen that hurts the eyes, knowing that all these things could be done in half the time without a computer.

The remaining bio-dynamic computer peripherals can be divided into two main groups. On the one hand we have the

Definition of owners of 'home' and 'semi-professional' computers

A male being who doesn't mind sacrificing endless hours on an activity which is of no practical use, thereby losing his grip on reality so that he no longer has time for his surroundings, his fellow men, his friends or his family.

In contrast to this we have the

A computer only crashes when the text
has not been saved for a long time.

Definition of owners of 'professional' computers

A male being who doesn't mind sacrificing endless hours on an activity which is of no practical use, thereby losing his grip on reality so that he no longer has time for his surroundings, his fellow men, his friends or his family.

Rosemary's two laws of suspected temptation
1 When a man begins to make remarks like 'We live in an Age of Information', he's going to buy a computer.
2 If he doesn't say this he has already ordered it.

Barbara's axiom of the three levels of problem solving
A computer freak deals with a problem in three different ways:
1 Where's the problem? I can't see it. Leave me alone.
2 I enjoy puzzling over almost insoluble problems. Leave me alone.
3 Call that a problem? No, I haven't solved it, it was too boring for me. Leave me alone.

The financial observation

Nobody needs a computer. But no computer user will ever dare admit that the whole thing was an expensive mistake.

Expanded laws by the author's wife
1   Men love computers because computers do
    what they are told. On the other hand, it
    doesn't matter whether that's what they actu-
    ally want to do.
2   'They' means men as well as computers.

Don's rule of the expert

When computer experts claim that the public
should understand computers, they really
mean that the public should accept computers
as God-given and not make such a fuss
but just let computer freaks do what they
want without interference from the outside
world.

Jennifer's dinner party lament
If you find yourself at a dinner party sitting
between the only two men who seem interesting, they will turn out to be computer freaks and
will talk about sort algorithms for hours on
end—and not even look at you.

Jennifer's expanded dinner party lament
If you then enrol on a computing course, at the
next dinner party you will find yourself sitting
between two men who are talking about stamp
collecting and who heartily disapprove of computers.

Platt's first computer law

It doesn't matter why people actually buy computers. Give them a week and they will be playing Space Invaders 26 hours a day.

Thoughts of a word processing romantic
1   The only reason why a computer freak needs a word processing program is to send you a copy of a standard love letter.
2   The length of letters sent to you is in inverse proportion to the number of program functions available and fonts installed.

The time-saved paradox
1   The time a computer freak saves through automation of tasks is in inverse proportion to the length of the programming.

The time saved T can be expressed by the following formula:
$$T = 1/1 + (P * F)$$
where P is the time needed for programming and F the frequency of the task. At best you will not save anything.
2   A computer freak will use the time when the computer is working automatically to sit and watch it, in order to make sure that it is working properly.

The feminist computer approach

Storage space and virility have one thing in common: The size is actually not very important but no man will admit this.

C LOSERS

The computer industry is a conspiratorial community. Programmers, freaks and both hardware and software manufacturers have conspired against users. Users, freaks and programmers have conspired against hardware and software manufacturers. Freaks, users and hardware and software manufacturers have conspired against programmers. And all of them in turn have conspired against the rest of humanity, who only know that a computer takes up space on the desk.

Of course no one can win this eternal struggle. Or to be more precise: no human being can win. Naturally, that leaves the computer, with its treachery locked into its bits and strip conductors, as the gleeful third party that gets off scot-free.

The basic observation made by all those affected by EDP—in short, all losers—is the

Basic observation of EDP application

A computer exists to relieve you of all the work which you wouldn't have had without it.

1 Programmers

Programmers (despite reports to the contrary) are people who, at dead of night, use unreliable hardware with totally unsuitable development packages for incompatible systems, to convert contradictory requests from incompetent operators into a program which no one will use anyway.

Programmers can be divided into two categories. The first, because they have far too little money and the expenses are far too great, fail in the attempt to play off against each other the logic errors of programming languages, the errors of compilers and the silicon-based inconsistencies of hardware developers, so that the computer system ends up doing more or less what it is expected to do. The other sort do all this for free.

A programmer's thinking is generally logical ('IF 1=2 CALL Mainprogram'), always structured ('ON Hunger GOSUB Aldi ELSE RETURN') and quite untainted by prejudice of any kind. Although there will always be the odd one who falls into the trap of thinking that the computer was created to serve man. Instead of the other way round.

Or, as the famous Anglo-American author

William D. Base Shakespeare said: 2b .or..not. 2b.

Although it is difficult to describe Murphy's Computer Law from a programmer's point of view (after all, a programmer is basically a completely superfluous link in the chain of marketing department-advertising department-programmer-sales department-user-support services-update department), an attempt will be made to do just this in the following pages. Even though software firms and users have agreed for years that life would be very much simpler without overpaid programmers and their objections to the feasibility of certain programming requests.

Consequently, well-known manufacturers have for some time been successfully developing their software directly by means of 'CASE' ('Computer Aided Software Engineering'), because in the end only a computer can write programs in such a way that other computers can misunderstand them properly.

Luke's basis for programming

It won't work.

First derivation
If it does work, then someone else has written it.

Second derivation
Swearing is the only language in which all programmers are completely proficient.

Conclusion
A computer will do what you program it to do—not what you want it to do.

Double rule for programming as a hobby

1   If you write a program yourself, the first time you run it you will come across an obvious error.
2   You will not be able to spot serious errors, though everyone else will notice them when your program starts.

Alec's observation on debugging

Nothing improves a program so much as errors from checking routines.

Alec's expanded observation
If debugging is the process by which errors are removed from a program, then programming is the process by which they are built in.

Alec's conclusion
If you don't know what you are doing, do it with panache.

First basis of EDP specialisation

Every developer who comes from out of town is an expert.

Second basis of EDP specialisation

An expert is anyone who knows more and more about less and less, until in the end he knows absolutely everything about absolutely nothing.

Clarke's sequence of software development

1 It is impossible—so I'm not going to waste my time on it.
2 It is possible, but not worth it.
3 I've had this wonderful idea.
4 Can anyone tell me why the competition beat us to it again?

Murgatroyd's memory axiom

The program code tends to fill up completely all regular memory available and then exceed it.

The Cerberus expansion
If you erase all comment lines and program an elaborate program routine in a new and quicker way, the program will actually be longer, need more memory, be too big for the compiler and will not work any more.

Laws of the study

1 All flat surfaces will be covered in junk in a very short time.

2 The disks will be underneath it.
3 The urgently needed trouble-shooting manual is nowhere to be found.
4 Cigarette ash and coffee will get into everything.

Insurance against catastrophe

Anyone who smiles when something goes wrong knows someone he can blame it on.

The eight cast-iron customer laws

1 A customer never knows how much a project will cost, only how much he will save by it.
2 When you have successfully expanded a program, the customer no longer wants it.
3 No customer knows what he really wants.
4 Every customer knows what he doesn't want.
5 No customer wants what you have already done.
6 But he doesn't know what he wants instead.
7 The customer who pays the least moans the most.
8 The customer will always demand bigger changes when a product has just been delivered.

Mnemonic of the time delay bug

1 You won't discover the critical error until the program has been error-free for six months.
2 This error will have distorted or destroyed the data which is important to the program so that it is no longer recoverable.

3   Meanwhile, the sort code cannot be found.

Peter's law of the spaghetti code

The program becomes more and more complicated until it exceeds the capabilities of the programmer who has to develop it further.

The expansion of Peter's law
The groundwork is always done by people who thus achieve the highest level of their incompetence.

The analysis axiom

After careful analysis of the structure of the program and excessive outlay, it will be discovered that it is the wrong program and cannot be used in solving the task.

Premise of invariable stress

Effort multiplied by time = constant.

First deduction from the stress premise
When you have enough time, you will not make enough effort.

Second deduction from the stress premise
The closer the time available gets to zero, the closer the effort gets to infinity.

Third deduction from the stress premise
Without the 'last minute' you would never finish anything.

General law of ideas

a) You never have time to do it right, but you have all the time you need to do it again.
b) Everything that is changeable on the directory of a program will take so long to change that it will be too late to change anything else on the program itself.

Roger's laws of debugging

1 In every program errors tend to appear at opposite ends of your error search.
2 When a listing contains an error, it looks error free.
3 When an error has been discovered and corrected, it becomes evident that it is already too late.
4 If it isn't too late, then the correction was wrong and the original text was right.

Conclusion 1
Since the correction was incorrect, it will be impossible to reinstate the original.

Conclusion 2
Given two possible mishaps, only the one that can be traced back to you will happen.

The quality syndrome

Every program that begins well ends badly. A project whose programming begins badly, ends dreadfully.

Conclusion 1

What appears to be simple is difficult. What appears to be difficult is impossible. What appears to be impossible even the cleaning lady can solve without a computer.

Conclusion 2

There is no such thing as a point beyond which things can get no worse.

Conclusion 3

The cleaning lady started working as a systems programmer for the competition long ago.

Will's principle of least amazement

When something has been done in one place in one way, then it must always be done in this way wherever it occurs.

The software team deduction

When it comes to solving problems in the programming, everyone in the software team has at least one plan which will not work.

The law of routines

1   If an error can creep into a program routine, it will.
2   There are errors even in routines which must be error free.

First conclusion
Every error is situated where it will take longest to find and where it will do the most damage.

Second conclusion
No error appears until the whole program has run through the last check.

Third conclusion
If the error is discovered earlier, the cause cannot be found.

Law of completion

Completion of a program always takes twice as long as planned. If this law is taken into consideration in the schedule, then the law of recursion will come into effect (see p. 78).

The adaptation theorem

Adapting a program to run on another computer system makes it unable to run on the computer for which it was originally written. Any attempt to adapt it for the first computer means that the program will not run on either.

The multiplication theory

The number of people on a programming team tends to increase, irrespective of the quantity of work available.

Amendment
If you do someone a favour, you will immediately become permanently responsible for that task.

Robin's limit regulation

The minimum requirements in program specification are also the maximum levels of performance that are possible on the model of computer you want.

Hogg's instability factor
Lack of clarity is of unalterable size.

Law of changing the program

The simpler an alteration seems to be, the bigger the repercussions and the more routines have to be rewritten.

Simplified deductions
1 Where there's a will, there's also a 'no way'.
2 There is nothing so simple that it cannot be done wrong.

The rule of interception

When you develop a routine to intercept obvious errors before printing, there will always be users who can get to this faulty data first by circumventing the interception routine.

Research axiom
The information which is most urgently needed is the least accessible.

Law of the resourcefulness of the user

When it is discovered that there are four possibilities for making a program crash and all four have been eliminated, the first person to use it will find a fifth.

Generalisation
You can make every program foolproof, but not that bloody foolproof.

The law of documentation

No one reads the manual.

Exceptions
1 Bad manuals will be read by editors doing a test report.
2 Only those sections in the manual will be read, which cause the user to get it wrong.
3 Every manual is obsolete before it goes to press.

Axiom of the manual/program relationship

When you clarify something so that no one can misunderstand it, somebody still will.

Bird's correlation between the test report and the manual

1 If you write a good manual, it is not detailed enough for the editor reporting on it.
2 If you write a good and detailed manual, manuals will not be assessed during the test.
3 If you write a bad manual, it will be the decisive criterion for the test reports in all computer magazines.

Daniel's laws on test reports

1 Your program will not be tested by computer magazines until rival products, which are better, are launched.
2 If clause 1 does not apply, the test editor will claim that the outstanding features of your program are not needed.
3 If clauses 1 and 2 do not apply, the test editor has not noticed the outstanding features in your program.

Daniel's deduction

1 Your program will always come off worst.
2 Your toughest rival always gets the best test results.
3 The more important the magazine running the tests is to the envisaged target group, the more catastrophic the evaluation.

Dogma of the cunning algorithm

If a program works, then something must have gone wrong previously.

Conclusions from the dogma of the cunning algorithm

a) It doesn't really matter what has gone wrong, it will look right.
b) Anyone you ask to help will not notice the error.
c) Anyone giving unsolicited advice will see it at once.
d) It doesn't matter what goes wrong, there is always someone there who knew it would.
e) Don't believe in miracles—depend on them.

The Templeton observation on elegant programming

Complex problems have simple, easily applied solutions—which are wrong.

Generalisation
The short cut is the longest distance between two points.

Positive exception
A good solution can be used on practically any problem. However, this will change both the problem and the solution for the worse.

General algorithm theories

1 Every formula and every constant must be considered as variables.
2 The essential dimension of an algorithm has the best chance of being left out and/or forgotten.

3 As soon as a program module works perfectly, it will become incompatible with the other modules.
4 Nothing ends as planned.
5 In any given task which contains n equations, undoubtedly there will be $n+1$ hidden unknowns.

Theoretical law of programming language compatibility (made world-famous under the name 'Turbo- . . . /Quick- . . . Axiom')

1 Thesis: Even if all the programming languages in the world are successfully replaced by one single uniform programming language, there will always be manufacturers who will bring out a separate, special version of this single uniform programming language.
2 Antithesis: This special version will only be compatible with itself.
3 Synthesis: This incompatibility will naturally extend to the various numbers of the same special version.

Practical application of programming language compatibility
1 Since there is no single uniform programming language, the confusion is total.
2 You are the one who will have to carry the can.

The 90-90-10 regulation of programming projects

1 The first 90 per cent of the program needs 10 per cent of the time available.
2 The remaining 10 per cent of the program needs 90 per cent of the time available.
3 You always start with the 10 per cent.

Consequent customer deduction from the 90-90-10 regulation
The 10 per cent you started with belongs to the program routines which the customer eventually wants to have taken out again.

Grey's law of programming

The same amount of time is allowed for running through n +1 unimportant tasks as for n tasks.

The expanded Evans-Henryson relationship of imprecision

Of the three parameters, time, money and task, you can only ever calculate two correctly at the same time:
1 If the task and the amount of time available for running through it are known, then it is impossible to calculate just how expensive it will all be.
2 If the budget and the amount of time available for running through the task are known, then no one will know which part of the task has to be solved.

3   If the task and also the budget available for running through it are known, then no one will know if or when you will ever finish it.
4   Anyone who can set all three parameters doesn't deal with problems.

Troubleshooting hypothesis
1   Exceptions are basically more numerous than rules.
2   There are exceptions to all known exceptions.
3   When you finally get to grips with the exceptions, you can no longer remember the rules for which they are valid.

Law of annoyances

As soon as you have erased a file in the belief that you will never need it again, you immediately need it.

The law of compiler and structure

The more structure commands you use in your program, the fewer your compiler will translate.

Supplement to the law of compiler and structure
Only the structures which contain errors will be translated.

First expansion of the law of compiler and structure
If a compiler accepts a program on the first run-

through without errors, the finished program will not deliver the output you wanted.

Second expansion of the law of compiler and structure
If you do without structured programming the compiler will produce incomprehensible error messages. You will not find the errors they refer to in your spaghetti code.

The law of character conversion

a) You can change capital letters into small letters and small letters into capital letters. As a result you will always get a text in which half the small letters are written as capitals and half the capital letters are written as small letters.
b) You cannot restore the original version.
c) You can only get an accurate text if you write it out by hand.
d) All things considered, it's easier to type in the whole text again.

Frank's observation of flowers

It doesn't matter what you use to water the flowers: half of it will always drip on to the listings.

Hal's command axiom

A command can never be so short that you can't include at least three typing errors.

Supplement to Hal's command axiom (also called the either-'<'-or-'#'-law)
If you type in a command without errors, you will instead insert a '<', a '#' or a '+' between the command and the final return.

Observation of an applications programmer
Principle: A user always does the wrong thing.
1 If you write 'type (Y) or (N)', he will type '(Y) or (N)'
2 If you write 'Press (RETURN)', he will type '(RETURN)'
3 If you write 'Press any key', he will either press SHIFT or activate the NUMLOCK key.

Martin's index observation
1 If you save something in an index file and you remember exactly what you saved there, you will forget the index file.
2 If you remember the index file, then you will no longer need the contents.

The Friday–Monday rule

A program which you erase on Friday will still be there on Monday.

The three fundamental software company errors

1 The more ambitious the programmer's plan, the later will fundamental development errors be discovered.

2 When a problem has disappeared, there are still people working on the solution.
3 The more people assigned to an overdue programming project, the more its completion is delayed.

The software observation
Urgency is inversely proportional to importance.

Basis of software engineering
Time eats money.

Daniel's lament of the last straw
There are two ways to write error-free programs.
But only the third one works.

2 Users

A user is generally defined as one of the computer peripherals who, equipped with completely inadequate hardware and an incomprehensible program, tries to solve a problem which would only take half the time without a computer. This definition is, however, extremely inexact and superficial. In reality a user is a computer peripheral who, equipped with completely inadequate hardware and an incomprehensible program, tries to solve a problem which wouldn't have existed without the computer.

This task will be made easier for the user by
— a well-written program version,
— user-friendly hardware as well as
— extensive and contradictory documentation.

A well-written program version usually comes with a badly printed manual, garbled systems messages and confused commands.

User-friendliness means polite, accommodating and tolerant behaviour on the part of the user, but insolent, incomprehensible and inflexible behaviour on the part of the hardware and software. The user is not supposed to develop ways of solving problems, but primarily to find out why the program and the hardware don't do what the user guides say they will.

Although Murphy's Computer Law is generally valid, it is not too difficult in theory for the user to unravel the tangled ways of hardware and software. That nobody in the history of the computer has yet done this does not conclusively disprove this statement.

Although it is difficult to describe Murphy's Computer Law from the user's point of view (after all, a user is basically a completely superfluous link in the chain of developer-programmer-manufacturer-user-repair service-scrap merchant) an attempt will be made to do just this in the following pages. Even though developers, programmers and manufacturers have agreed for years that life would be very much simpler without users.

Consequently, well-known manufacturers have for some time been successfully developing their hardware and software without taking this error-laden link in the chain into consideration.

First basis of computer use

When anything goes wrong, all you know is that you have made an odd number of errors.

Second basis of computer use

The number of errors n in any computer system or any program package can be calculated precisely by the following formula:

$$n > a$$

where a is any given number.

Third basis of computer use

If nothing goes wrong the number of errors is bigger

$$n + 1$$

Fourth basis of computer use

If all else fails, read the instructions.

Propagation of problems axiom

Inside every big problem is a little one trying to get out.

Shawcross's inversion
Inside every small problem there is a big one trying to get out.

The author's last straw lament
Even where there is no problem at all, there is a big one trying to get out.

Law of the statistical logic of software manufacturers

According to market research, 80 per cent of users only use 20 per cent of the functions.

First logical deduction
20 per cent of users need the 80 per cent

of functions which their program doesn't possess.

Second logical deduction
You can be 100 per cent certain that you belong to this 20 per cent.

Clarification
A programmer would be the last person to use his program.

Theorem of program use

What you want to do with a program
—is not in the manual
—will only be explained in the updated manual
—will only be implemented in the next version of the program.

Law of maximisation of cost and time

Every urgent programming job costs more and takes longer.

Expansion
Every program costs more and takes longer—with every run-through.

The four program ground rules

1 All programs that run without errors are obsolete.
2 All useful programs are changed.
3 All absurd features are immediately incorporated.

4   All errors are immediately installed as new
    functions.

Generalisation
By the time you have understood something, it
is obsolete.

Laws of buying computers

1   Manufacturers' claims about performance
    should be multiplied by a factor of 0.5.
2   Users' demands on performance should be
    multiplied by a factor of 0.25.
3   Accompanying manuals and systems disks
    are filed away in sub post offices and cannot
    be found.
4   When, after a long search, you finally buy
    your computer, it will be half the price the
    following week. Alternatively, a model will
    appear which will offer twice the perform-
    ance for the same price.

Deductions from the guarantee
1   Claims under the guarantee become invalid
    as soon as you pay the bill.
2   A 180-day guarantee guarantees only one
    thing: that the equipment will go wrong on
    day 181.

Axiom of the futility of error-removal

When you have perfected a work-around for a
program error, a new version will appear in
which the error has been rectified.

Axiom of the futility of memory expansion

The main memory of every computer is too small. If you expand your system, a new version of your program will appear which needs at least 10K more memory than you have gained as a result of your expansion.

The author's first computer show law (also known as the 'NEC-Earl's Court axis'):

Two consecutive appointments at a computer show are at places as far apart as possible.

Deduction 1
There is never an official show bus operating between the two places.

Exception
Two consecutive appointments are at the same place only when you are urgently called away after the first one to somewhere which is the greatest possible distance away.

Deduction 2
When you are on the way from one place to another, inevitably you bump into a business partner well-known for his talkativeness.

Deduction 3
The two most interesting presentations at the show take place at the same time in different halls.

The author's second computer show law

You will never get to an appointment on time.

Expansion of the author's second computer show law
a) If you get there too early, the person you were going to talk to has cancelled the appointment without telling you.
b) If you fall over yourself to get there on time, you have to wait for ever.
c) If you get there too late, you get there too late.

The author's third computer show law

The manufacturer whose stand you most want to visit at the show has cancelled at such short notice that it was too late to change the catalogue.

Exception to the author's third computer show law
The manufacturer is represented but he is not displaying the product you are interested in, or the only person on the stand who knows anything about the product is taken ill before the show starts.

Axiom of error optimisation

If you run a program and it's error-free, don't worry. It can't last.

Conclusions from the axiom of error optimisation

1 When things can't get any worse, they will.
2 When you think that the error has been rectified and the program is run again, you will
   have overlooked something.
3 If a chain of events can go wrong, it will go
   wrong in the worst possible sequence.
4 When it has gone wrong, it will happen again.
5 When the worst that can happen has happened, it has just happened to someone you
   know—only much worse.

Observation on computer publishing

Computer publishers produce computer books
in which they explain what you have not understood in computer magazines. And vice versa.

Consequent conclusion to the observation on computer publishers
You don't understand either of them.

The triple law of test reports in computer magazines

1 The test report on the program you are interested in appears a week after you have
   bought it.
2 The program you have bought always gets
   the worst possible assessment.
3 The program that you almost bought gets the
   best write-up.

The 12 advice fallacies for the gullible buyer
(also known as the 'What-the-salesman-said-in-answer-to-the-critical-question law'):

1   'It was working yesterday.'
2   'We sold out of the computer this runs on ten minutes ago.'
3   'This section of the program isn't actually on this hard disk now.'
4   'You can easily get round this problem if you restructure the work routine in your business a little.'
5   'I have only worked with this program for two days.'
6   'Of course it can be expanded. We've done it dozens of times already.'
7   'Our expert in that field is on holiday at the moment.'
8   'We only have the demonstration version of the program, but the new version is on its way.'
9   'We only have the demonstration version of the program, but the new version is error-free.'
10 'When you have been using the program/computer/peripheral in your business for a couple of weeks, you will be able to deal with the questions yourself.'
11 'Of course we have an after sales service.'
12 'No, at this price there are no hidden costs.'

D OBSERVATIONS

Over the years particular observations, ground rules or philosophies have been developed in every area of life. EDP is no exception. In the following pages the author has collected together the most important examples.

Although these truths and observations sometimes sound defeatist, the reader should not be deterred. It all comes down to the

Basic observation of EDP

There are only two incontrovertible observations in life:
1 Computers need people.
2 The earth is flat.

Ground rule of all computer users

Do not let anything mechanical know that you are in a hurry.

The programmers' inspiration

An error-free program is like squaring the circle. Everyone thinks it can be done but no one has seen it.

Margaret's observation
The probability of such a thing happening is in inverse proportion to the wish.

The computer kids' lament (with apologies to Bob Marley)
No Woman, No Cray.

The architects' and programmers' observation

If architects designed buildings like programmers write their programs, a single woodpecker could destroy whole towns.

God's objection
If God had meant humans to use computers He would have given them 16 fingers.

Ben's holiday destination
The bigger the island of knowledge, the longer the coast of despair.

Law of logic

Those who use computers shouldn't be surprised that when they put garbage in they get garbage out.

Expanded law of logic
'Artificial intelligence' ('AI') has about as much in common with intelligence as 'manufactured flavourings' ('YUK') have with natural flavours.

The author's philosophy

Reloading programs into the computer is faster than going to the trouble of having to switch it off and on again.

On the writing of programs

Writing programs is like writing novels. First you have to think of a couple of characters and then you have to see how you get on with them.

First comment of the author's wife
At least this way a man has someone to obey his every word.

Second comment of the author's wife
Computers are unreliable, just like people. But computers are considerably more thorough.

Mike's praise of programmers
At last, a language without a pluperfect.

Law of the error

All major discoveries were made because of errors.

Conclusion from the law of the error
All errors end with the discovery of an error.

Conclusion from the conclusion from the law of errors
The discovery of an error is the basis of the next more serious error.

Observation from the test laboratory

Under carefully controlled conditions of temperature, humidity, pressure and other variables, the computer will do exactly what it wants.

Binomial rule

God created all numbers, Man did the rest.

The data bank dilemma

If you have bought an address management program which will comfortably manage 500 addresses, you will discover that you don't know that many people.

The intoxication of speed

A computer can do with breathtaking speed a great many things which probably never needed doing in the first place.

Sysop's lament
Undeclared identifier(s): 'Women', 'Girls'.

The final consequence

The error message is your computer's most common revenge.

E HOARY OLD COMPUTER MYTHS

Fairy tales and legends have always aided mankind in explaining inexplicable events. In ancient history there were gods and spirits which could be blamed for all the injustices that plagued the working man. Today, in our enlightened Age of Information, IBM, Microsoft, Apple and Ashton-Tate have taken their place.

But in spite of these attempts to explain the nature of hardware and software there is still room for numerous other myths which have persisted for decades in the world of the computer user.

The filing myth

The installation of computers in the office will make the use of paper superfluous.

The first analog myth

Computers make people superfluous.

The second analog myth

Computers make anything superfluous.

The user myth

Somewhere there is user-friendly software.

The book myth

There is an easily understandable computer manual which will enable me to solve all my problems.

The CCITT myth

We shall soon have standardised interfaces.

The hardware myth

It would be better to wait a couple of years until computers have really improved.

The IBM myth

The IBM Standard has been successful because it has developed farthest technically.

The information myth

You can get information from on-line data banks.

The integration myth

Integrated user packages have expanded to include all requirements.

The compatibility myth

A PC which is 100 per cent IBM-compatible.

The laptop myth

The person who works with a laptop in a plane causes the latter (not the former) to crash.

The solution myth (1)

Every problem can be solved by computers.

The solution myth (2)

My problem can be solved by computers.

The solution myth (3)

Anybody's problem can be solved by computers.

The network myth

We shall soon have a valid network-standard.

The price myth

It would be better to wait a couple of years until computers are cheaper.

The professionalism myth

Professional users definitely need an IBM-compatible computer.

The rationalisation myth

Computers simplify every task.

The software myth

It would be better to wait a couple of years until software has really improved.

The Unix myth

The manufacturers will agree on a common Unix standard.

The virus myth

No viruses can get into my PC.

The timesaving myth

If you have a laptop you can work when the office is closed.

F THE BEST EXCUSES

As we have already discovered, computers have not been introduced into offices and businesses because they work faster or better. Anyone who works with a computer will know at once that computers on the one hand, and effective work on the other, are mutually incompatible.

And so we have

The department-specific deduction of the double law of complex hardware

If you want a permanent excuse in your department for any errors, you must equip yourself with a computer.

Basically there is no better excuse for errors, problems and missed deadlines than a resident computer.

So that a user can have the correct excuse to hand without having to spend a long time searching for it, we have collected together the following most credible excuses.

The general excuse

'It's not in my manual.'

The expanded general excuse
'Someone has borrowed my manual.'

The general computer excuse (version 1)

'My PC is not compatible enough for that.'

The general computer excuse (version 2)

'My PC is too compatible for that.'

The print-out excuse

'My paper feed is not working properly.'

The business graphics excuse

'My plotter pens have dried up.'

The data file excuse (1)

'My hard disk is full.'

The data file excuse (2)

'My hard disk is too slow for that.'

The data file excuse (3)

'My hard disk has suddenly developed defective sectors.'

The printer excuse (1)

'My ribbon has run out.'

The printer excuse (2)

'I haven't got the right drive.'

The printer excuse (3)

'My printer doesn't recognise this character setting.'

The obvious excuse

'It was working earlier.'

The not-so-obvious excuse

'Mrs X always does that for us.'

The quite obvious excuse

'Nobody told me which way up the keyboard goes.'

The installation excuse

'My resident storage programs have cancelled each other out.'

The interface excuse

'The printer adaptation is still not working.'

The linguistic excuse

'In the past we have always written programs in another language.'

The mailbox excuse

'That isn't consistent with my terminal emulation.'

The on-line excuse

'I have forgotten my password.'

The program excuse (1)

'My working memory is too small for this program.'

The program excuse (2)

'This isn't consistent with EMS.'

The program excuse (3)

'I haven't got the newest version of the program yet.'

The programmer's excuse

'Ask the developer when he comes.'

The memory excuse

'Someone's written on this disk in ballpoint pen.'

The drawing program excuse

'I've got the wrong graphics card.'

The publisher's excuse

'Your royalty cheque is in the post.'

G FAMOUS LAST WORDS

The last words of great men (and women) on their deathbed have been handed down as immortal *bons mots*. Considerably more mundane—but just as immortal—are the last words of ordinary computer users.

Compared to Goethe's demand for 'More light', is there not more drama in the do-it-yourself hardware enthusiast's question as to whether the cable he is about to solder is live? In this case, of course, only if his (last) question can be answered in the affirmative by the bystanders . . .

'I don't think this cable is live.'

'I'll just finish writing this procedure before I save it.'

'The manufacturer says these two expansion cards work together.'

'In the computer magazine it says that nothing can happen to you if you tinker with this hardware.'

'I don't think this program contains a virus.'

'Turn it off if you want, I've saved the text.'

'This diskette does not contain any important data files.'

'You can erase the whole index. I've still got the files.'

'My hard disk is guaranteed virus-free.'

'Why should I make a backup before starting up the optimizer on the hard disk?'

'This drive tolerates this sort of handling.'

'I don't need a park program to move this computer.'

'My emergency power supply can easily cope with these power surges.'

'There is always enough power in the laptop's powerpack.'

'It doesn't matter if the computer crashes, the RAM on my laptop is battery-powered.'

'That must be where you unplug the printer.'

'Don't worry, you can leave the computer on in spite of the thunderstorm, we've got a good lightning conductor.'

'Mind you don't fall over that cable.'

Conclusion

In the struggle between you and the computer,
back the computer.

**Afterword
or:
Why everything is bound to go wrong
when you publish a Murphy book**

It is only natural, when you publish a book on Murphy's Law, that everything is bound to go wrong that can go wrong (and of course everything you think can't go wrong too). For it is well known that the only time murphyological aspects fail to appear is when you want to demonstrate them.

It was entirely predictable, for example, that the in-house marketing and technical feasibility study for this Murphy book (of which there is naturally only a single copy) would disappear without trace during the decision-making process and that it has still not reappeared. It was only natural, too, given the closing words of the preface, that in spite of a spell check program, typing errors still piled up in the manuscript of this book, resulting in the necessity for a second proof reading.

This allowed the author to realise that computer break-downs were not limited to hardware and software, but also extended logically to computer publishing and computer book authorship. In this connection the observations obtained range from

Sharp's telephone panic

The only number at the publisher's office which is permanently engaged is that of your editor.

to

Normal royalty statement logic

Between the signing of your contract and your first royalty payment the person responsible will have moved to another department, and his successor will know nothing about it.

With the attempt to subject electronic data processing to a murphyological examination the author has thrown down a challenge to the maliciousness embedded in silicon and the program lines of his own computer and the program he uses. Only in this way can the accumulation of murphyological events be understood, to be combined with a clear conscience in the

Meta observation of murphyological research (also known as 'Dr Hardacre's Law')

You will experience the best murphyologies when your Murphy manuscript is at the printers and you can't add any more to it.

So all that remains for the author to do is to carry on with his Murphy research and before too long to publish newly acquired observations in an expanded volume. In the end insidiousness-

137

chips and perfidy-programs don't just lurk in computers, but in all modern office and communications facilities. Anyone who has tried even once to carry on an important telephone conversation, to copy an important presentation correctly or to send a really urgent document by fax, knows where the idea comes from.

This all-pervading power of electronic breakdown can only be thoroughly documented through solidarity and co-operation between all the people involved (for 'people' read 'losers'). If you come across a murphyological law that you cannot find in this book, write to me care of the publishers. If your letter reaches me (you know why I doubt whether it will, don't you?), I shall gladly include your observation in my next book on the 'Murphy' theme. Perhaps I shall also succeed in persuading the publishers that they should reward the contributor of every murphyological law printed with a copy of this new work (I know why you doubt whether this will happen).

Joachim Graf